JESUS: MORE THAN A SUPERSTAR

JESUS: MORE THAN A SUPERSTAR

DR. OLUSOLA FADARE

ReadersMagnet, LLC

JESUS: MORE THAN A SUPERSTAR
Copyright © 2023 by Dr. Olusola Fadare

Published in the United States of America
ISBN   Paperback: 979-8-89091-149-0
ISBN   eBook: 979-8-89091-150-6

All rights reserved. No part of this publication may be reproduced, stored in a retrieval system or transmitted in any way by any means, electronic, mechanical, photocopy, recording or otherwise without the prior permission of the author except as provided by USA copyright law.

The opinions expressed by the author are not necessarily those of ReadersMagnet, LLC.

ReadersMagnet, LLC
10620 Treena Street, Suite 230 | San Diego, California, 92131 USA
1.619. 354. 2643 | www.readersmagnet.com

Book design copyright © 2023 by ReadersMagnet, LLC. All rights reserved.

Cover design by Tifanny Curaza
Interior design by Dorothy Lee

TABLE OF CONTENTS

Acknowledgements 7
Dedication 9
Introduction 11
Jesus! More Than A Superstar 13
More About… Jesus 16
Nothing Can Compare To The Christian Faith 19
The Greatest Sermon Ever Preached 22
Practical Christianity 24
Practical Christianity 27
Understanding God 30
Holiness! Just What 33
Does It Mean? 33
Holy Living And Deliverance 35
More On Holiness 37
Consecration Or Compromise? 40
Resurrection Power Is In The Air 43
Blessed 46
America! Church Or Convenience? 50
Of Light Weights And The Skillful 54
Religion 58
Book Summary 61

ACKNOWLEDGEMENTS

Thank you, Stacey Gregory, for bringing my writing together into this wonderful book formation. I could not have done this without your support and knowledge.

DEDICATION

This book is dedicated to all believers in Christ who are open- minded to the truth and always eager to have more of Jesus and everything that challenges a parochial knowledge of the Godhead as they expand their spiritual horizon.

INTRODUCTION

You have in this book a wide variety of subjects. Some are practical teachings straight from the scriptures. Some are what you could call sermons, while some are what look like religious essays that are based on observation of a sad reality or attitudes that we see around in worshiping and serving God, which is devoid of zeal, truth, spirit, and spiritual hunger.

If you wanted to view these pieces as a genre, the appropriate one would be SERMONS, as they bear similarities in form and subject matter, though not necessarily in style.

Do not read it as a narrative because each piece is titled differently as different as the contents of each. Yet it will be better read chapter by chapter, and prayerfully too, with a grave and humble approach so as to benefit the reader. Some will make you pause and ponder or check the scripture for reference. Still, it could be read relaxing on your bed, couch, or while waiting in line indoor or outdoor with serious- mindedness. You should enjoy reading it when in transit, provided you are not the one driving.

Passing it on to a friend, church member, or neighbor to read will not only be advised but can generate healthy and beneficial discussions. Of course, readers can always contact the author by e-mail or by phone for discussions and questions.

Dr. Olu Fadare

olusolafad@aol.com

9175355462

USA

JESUS! MORE THAN A SUPERSTAR

PASTOR FADARE

I never watched the 1973 movie Jesus Christ Superstar. Neither the 1996 revival version of the rock opera, produced by Andrew Webber and Tim Rice. There was also the 80's American version. What I remember was my disdain for the title. I thought it was a secular movie - a Broadway show. It was. While the secular commentators raved over it, a North Carolina resident, presumably a Christian, was quoted describing it as a "blasphemous piece of well-crafted trash."

One of the movie's creators, Tim Rice, earlier mentioned, opinionated that the Bible's characterization of Judas Iscariot is a cardboard cut-out figure of evil. Rice's mission was to humanize Judas. To us believers, that mission was a monumental failure. It is blasphemous to call, describe or depict our Lord Jesus Christ, a superstar. It is blasphemy to call him a celebrity. The world has its stars, celebrities, and superstars. Their own "Jesus" is one of them. So much about the secular world. The Islamic religion sees Jesus as a prophet of God, nothing more. That is true but is a half-truth. He was a prophet and much more than a prophet. Jesus Himself introduced John the Baptist to his audience (Luke 7:19 28). John had sent two of his disciples to find out from Jesus if He was Jesus. What a humble Jesus is our savior. John did not see the pomp and pageantry, the sounding of trumpets, the pompous display of wealth, and the endless chants of Hosannah expected to characterize such a great ministry of Jesus. Moreover, he perhaps expected Jesus to descend with a bang on the Herodian royalty to deliver him from prison supernaturally. When the two disciples had left, Jesus began to talk about John. "But what made you went out to see? A Prophet? Yeah, I say unto you and much more than a prophet."

John was more than a prophet. He was the greatest prophet ever born. He was also the only and sole forerunner of Christ's incarnation. If a man described as the greatest prophet (John) was the one who at the beginning of Jesus' ministry introduced Jesus in John chapter 1:16-35 as the one who brought grace and truth. The only begotten Son who was in the bosom of God. The one who is preferred before me. The one whose shoe laces I am not worthy to untie. The Lamb of God who takes away the sin of the world. If all the aforementioned descriptions and witnesses of Jesus came from the greatest prophet on earth, then the person so described must be greater than the one who described him. This is where the religions of the world are faulty. Any religion is fundamentally faulty that does not: (1) acknowledge that Jesus is the Son of God (Matthew 16:16), the only begotten son of the father as described by John 1:18, (2) that teaches that salvation is not only by Jesus, and (3) that acknowledges Jesus as the Son of God and acknowledges and elevates another person or entity other than God, and the Holy Ghost. Simply put, there is no basis for comparing Jesus with any created being. Peter, in utter ignorance, tried it in Matthew 17 when Jesus was transfigured before Peter, James, and John. On that mountain of transfiguration, Jesus' face was that of the sun shining in its full strength, and His clothing was sparkling white as the light. Then suddenly, Moses and Elijah appeared to all four of them, and both talked to Jesus. Peter seized the opportunity of the great occasion to ask Jesus, "If you are willing, let us make three tabernacles, one for you, one for Moses, and one for Elijah, according to his own ranking. He might be right in ranking - Jesus first, followed by Moses, the great prophet of God and leader of the Israelites, and then Elijah, the fiery prophet. Yet Jesus cannot be grouped with these two heavenly saints. God heard in heaven and instantly corrected the great error. God could have said, "Shut up! Peter. This one Jesus is different. He is my beloved Son, in whom I am well pleased." And that was what God would have said in effect.

Not only do God and man acknowledge Jesus as the Son of God, even demons still do. Two of them in Matthew 8:28 saw Jesus and cried out, "What have we to do with You, Jesus, You SON OF GOD? Have you come here to torment us before our time?" So if God, man, and demons say Jesus is the only begotten Son of God, why will mortal unregenerated men reduce him to a prophet, celebrity, or superstar? The reason is that they are unregenerated. The writer of the Book of Hebrew contrasted Jesus with the Angels of God by asking a rhetorical question, "For unto which of the angels said he at anytime, Thou art my son, this day have I begotten thee?" Hebrew 1:5. The next verse is even written: "And let all the angels of God worship Him." The contrast continued in the next verse. Let the unbelieving and the unregenerated know that this Jesus is the express image of God, who is in the form of God and thought it not a robbery to be equal with God, but made Himself of no reputation, and took upon Him the form of a servant, and was made in the likeness of men... Philippians 2:6-9. A man of God once said that wrong doctrine would not make you to be what God wants you to be in the kingdom of God. Heresy will make you to be out of the kingdom altogether. It is heresy to equate Jesus with all His majesty, names (above all names), glory, place in the trinity with finite, mortal homo-sapiens. He is the Alpha and Omega, the ancient of days, the everlasting father, the mighty God, the prince of peace (Yeshua Shalom), the coming messiah.

Exercise for you reader: Where in the Bible did Jesus say?

"No one comes to the father but by me."

MORE ABOUT... JESUS
PASTOR FADARE

In my previous account, I made an apologetic case for Jesus as more than a superstar because of the blasphemous, uncharacteristic way He had been unequally co-ranked with the secular superstars of the world. This is Jesus, who the Bible writers could not even co-rank with Moses, nor even the Angels of God. If He were a star, He would undoubtedly be the supreme star. He created the stars. In fact, He had a star, as was seen by the Magi (Matthew 2:1-10). These wise men that saw His star were seeking him literally.

When Jesus started His ministry here on earth, men were still seeking Him. In Capernaum, where Jesus used as His headquarters, He taught, preached, and worked miracles. In Mark 1:33, it was recorded that all the city gathered at the door to hear him. He woke up very early in the morning, and sneaked out into a solitary place to pray. Simon Peter and some apostles traced His steps, so to speak, and upon locating him said: All men seek you. (Mark 1:37). The apostles sought him. All His disciples sought Him. All men sought Him. All men are still seeking Him today, figuratively speaking.

I think it expedient that all people should be seeking Jesus today. Let the whole world be caught up in the prevalent momentum of His imminent coming. I ran into a young lady right outside of my office building, sometime in the fall of 2018. With a pen in hand and pad or a notebook, she walked up to me and asked a couple of questions, one of which was: "How do you get to work, by your own car or public transportation?" I answered, "Both." She was doing a study either for the city of New York or for a college project. After her interview, I asked if I could ask my own questions and conduct my own short interview. She cracked up while giving a yes and nod. I asked who Jesus was as if she knew Jesus? Her countenance noticeably transformed from the light mood to the serious, "Jesus is the man everyone worships," she said almost authoritatively. "Are you among the everyone you just mentioned?" I asked politely. She smiled but never answered yes or no. I knew she was a Hindu worshipper. She did not deny it. Hours and days later, it was still amazing to hear from a Hindu teenager that Jesus is the man everyone worships. You can feel the air saturated with the name of Jesus. Jesus Himself has begun to appear to people of other religions, especially Muslims, more than at any time in the history of the world. It is the last of the last days.

When in the early 1980s, the Lord started to make Himself known to me, I initially did not know Him but knew about Him. I had not been truly born again, and I did not know that concept. Knowing God to me at that period of my life was tantamount to getting my wishes and needs met, and boy! were they met. If anyone had preached salvation to me at that time, I would have in my pride told him or her that I knew God more than that person. After all, I had meaningful dreams. I read the Bible and memorized some Psalms. It went on like that until the voice of God audibly woke me up from sleep one afternoon, "Son, let your gratitude (thankfulness) be more than your requests." I was scared but then knew how to thank and praise God henceforth. So when I truly got saved a few years after, my whole spiritual perspective changed. It was no more, give me this or I need that and this. I knew Christ more intimately as I grew in the faith, thanks to a steady prayer life, voracious reading and study of the word of God, uninterrupted church attendance, and corporate and personal evangelism. I loved the Lord, trusted Him, believed His word in the Bible from cover to cover and even in the cover itself. I also heard from God frequently in dreams and visions. Yet, I had at least two regrets. I will share one of them and leave the other for my next installment. Don't miss it.

What is my first regret? My regret was not living in the Bible, New Testament days, and getting to see Jesus physically. What a blessed generation that saw Him, touched Him, and heard Him. I thought I had missed a lot. What a miss!

I would have followed Him all day long, asked Him tons of questions, fetched Him water, worshiped and adored Him, and cherished His presence, His peace, and perfection all the time. He is adorable. His sweetness, gentleness, smile. His build, frame, figure, entire anatomy, the whole elements that constitute His physique and visage. What about His wise, efficacious words spoken with undiminished love and uncommon sense, like:

"Give unto Caesar the things that are Caesar's and to God the things that are God's."

"Blessed are the pure in heart for they shall see God."

"You are the salt of the earth."

"Come unto me ye that labor and are heavy laden and I shall give you rest."

I would have heard these eternal words rolling off from His lips. If you have that kind of regret, don't despair. By His spirit, the Lord Himself made me know that I have not missed a thing, neither you. Suppose you can only get intimate with Jesus. Suppose you can only make Him the center of everything in your life and make him first. As you make Him first, you are already making God first. You can come to Jesus, and He will take you to God, but you cannot get to God without going through Jesus (John 14:6). You can hear Jesus now more than if you had lived in His days. You can have more intimacy with Him now. You and I are more of a blessed generation. That's what the Lord is saying to you now. Seek Him with all your heart more and more.

NOTHING CAN COMPARE TO THE CHRISTIAN FAITH

THE TRUE WAY

with Dr. Olu Fadare

Unreserved glory to the Living God for the debut of this column which will appear once or twice a month. This column will mind its own business but will predictably also mind other people's business for them. Meaning, it will be committed to affirming and proclaiming the whole truth and nothing but the whole truth of the gospel and, in the process, might unwittingly step on people's toes. You will agree with me that truth to some people is relative. To some, they rightly believe truth is absolute, but their own idea of truth is diametrically opposed to the biblical data and declaration. How then on earth would such not have a deep-seated aversion to what will be coming out of this column?

Though this is not a secular column, neither will it tolerate secularism in any form, but it will engage as the need may be in secular discussions. After all, we all interact daily with the secular world. Yes, we do have secular jobs, and the fact that while Christians should not be unequally yoked with unbelievers (2 CORINTHIANS 6:14) we cannot, we should not, we ought not to avoid them like plagues. We must exude Gods love and invite them to Christ, the very personae of truth. This column will promote Christ Jesus above all religious and secular gods and heads of religions. Unfortunately, and to the detriment of their own personal relationship with Jesus, some of my brethren in faith compromise by (not necessarily believing) but saying that we all serve the same

God. They tend towards sympathy for these other religions and their adherents, especially when the adherents are friends or relatives.

This is not a clarion call to demonize, discriminate or be intolerant of other people and their religion, far from it. It is just a statement of the fact that there is only ONE WAY to God, and that is Jesus Christ. He made a self-declaration in John 14:6 – "I AM THE WAY, THE TRUTH AND THE LIFE; NO ONE COMES TO THE FATHER BUT BY ME."

Friend, do you know there is no head of any religion anywhere and anytime in the history of the world that made any such declaration? No, none. In fact the worshipers of Bhuda will tell you that it is the oldest religion on earth. Yet Bhuda on his death bed made his own declaration: "I AM STILL SEARCHING FOR THE TRUTH" My own thing is that we should respect and love all people. Jews or gentiles. Let those who wear Hijab wear it, and our friends their Yarmulka. We will love them the same. That is the essence of Christianity. Whatever practice that is repulsive, hateful and evil in any of the notable religions, this column will let out its voice against it.

As a theologian, preacher and pastor, I will continue to speak and preach against immoral and amoral behavior, against sin in the society and in the Church and my moral authority will continue to be the Bible. Having studied to some extent major World Religions, their beliefs, tenets and doctrines, I can assuredly say the Bible is the final authority. Simply, it is the WORDS OF GOD, breathed by, inspired by and largely dictated by God. It is JESUS in the written form. It is sacred, true and final. I believe it from cover to cover including the cover itself that reads " HOLY BIBLE. When God says, no one of it will pass without being fulfilled. He means it. Aside from the truth, which no other religion has been able to state categorically as their core doctrine, the biblical doctrine of eternal life is another unique one for the Christian faith. The Christian faith is the only faith that knows for certain where the truly born again believer is going after the earthly sojourn, and where the unregenerated and false prophets and false unrepentant

"Christians" will end their journey. Assuring all genuine children of God, the Bible says in First John (1 John 5:13), "These things have I written unto you that believe on the name of the Son of God that you may know that you have eternal life and that you may believe on the name of the Son of God."

THE GREATEST SERMON EVER PREACHED

By Pastor OLU FADARE

The last two sermons discussed the greatest and most crucial questions ever asked in the Bible and anywhere. In the same paradigm of the superlative, the greatest, most powerful sermon ever preached is the Sermon on the Mount. It is even a demerit to ordinarily call it "The Sermon on the Mount" as it is often referred to. A biblical and grammatical justice to the title would read like the title above, a most seldom-used reference. With this befitting title, the emphasis is deservedly on the most excellent sermon as opposed to the Mount. What is the most excellent sermon ever preached, and what makes it most powerful? Its power and greatness that where not derived from the fact that it was preached by Jesus Christ, our Lord. (He preached many more sermons, for that matter.) Its greatness and power are derived from:

1. Its profound and foundational truth
2. Its prolific nature, covering chapters 5 through 7 of Matthew's gospel, with the most minor chapter running 29 verses and the longest, 48 verses.
3. It's simple, though the not simplistic presentation is easily understandable.
4. One does not have to be a college student to understand its message. Neither does one have to be an English professor to laud the clarity of its diction and the conciseness of its expressions.

5. The entirety of the Sermon provides us with the pillars of the Christian faith and the bedrock of Paul's Sermon in Romans chapter 12. Talking about its profoundness and foundational truth, what can be more profound than believers being metaphorically referred to as the salt of the earth and the light of the world? (Matthew 5:13-14) And that except our righteousness exceeds that of the Pharisees, we shall in no way enter the kingdom of heaven (Mt. 5:20). Friends, what can be substituted for the truth - that Jesus did not come to destroy the law but to fulfill it? In other words, we will still have to keep the law of righteousness. It should be pointed out that this Sermon's inherent beatitudes is in the early verses of chapter 5.

6. The beatitudes are inter-connected, inter-related, and inter-dependent. "Blessed are they that mourn." (Verse 4) is related to "Blessed are they which are persecuted for righteousness sake. "Blessed are the poor in spirit, for theirs is the kingdom of heaven." (Verse 3) is related to and connected with verse 5, "Blessed are the meek for they shall inherit the earth." "Blessed are the merciful, for they shall obtain mercy" is dependent on verses 3 and 9 because it is hard to be merciful except when you have been genuinely born again, having experienced the mercy of God first, in forgiving your sins. For now, we will dwell on the beatitudes, starting from the first in the series: "Blessed are the poor in spirit, for theirs is the kingdom of heaven." This is the pillar of the beatitudes. Being poor in the spirit can be explained with this analogy: A person, who is poor financially, undoubtedly can most likely be characterized as humble. Many humble people are poor than are rich. Conversely, there are very few that are rich and still humble.

PRACTICAL CHRISTIANITY
THE GREATEST SERMON EVER PREACHED
BLESSED ARE THEY WHO HUNGER AND THIRST AFTER RIGHTEOUSNESS
By Pastor OLU FADARE

This is the fourth beatitude in the series. "'The greatest sermon ever preached." This is practical Christianity. Popular known as the Sermon on the Mount, they are by no means enticing words of men's wisdom. Men's wisdom or worldly wisdom is foolishness at its best and curse at its worst.

Blessed are they which do hunger and thirst after righteousness. It did not stop there. Like all the other beatitudes is, it has its own rider and unique blessing, for they shall be filled. Filled with what? Filled with righteousness, of course.

If our Lord Jesus Christ happened to show up bodily in one of His churches today to preach, He would undoubtedly lament the lethargy, the lack of hunger and thirst that has permeated the body of Christ. I am not alluding to those outside the church; whether backslidden or unsaved, I am talking about living churches. Have you noticed it? Have you spiritually discerned it, though you do not need the gift of discernment to know this? Or are you part of such lethargy?

One preacher said or wrote that holiness is what you are; righteousness is what you do. I agree. I believe we cannot separate righteousness from holiness. Have you ever heard of one who is holy and not righteous or vice versa? If one has a form of righteousness or godliness, and denies the power thereof, that one cannot live a holy life, he is not altogether righteous. Readers, friends, and brethren, my heart is burdened to hear brethren and even ministers in many churches hide under the cloak of the scripture in Romans 3:23 (For all have sinned and come short of the glory of God). They will never quote Romans 6:23 (For the wages of sin is death, but the gift of God is eternal life). So these people say we are all sinners. They justify their own unrighteousness. But the scripture is right that we have all sinned and come short of the glory of God.

When you have been truly born again, having truly repented, that is, expressed sorrow for your sins, made a commitment to say bye-bye to them, made a U-turn commitment to Jesus, and begin to obey and follow Him, being now your Lord. However, you have sinned in the past, and you are no more short of the glory of God. If you sin by chance, by mistake, or through carelessness and you go right before God, not run away from Him or hide your sin, God will forgive you. You cannot be labeled a sinner because of that.

A sinner is one who is practicing sin, wallowing in sin, or commits a premeditated (knowingly) sin and confesses it, goes right back and then confesses it again, and the unending cycle becomes a continuum of play game. If you fall into the category of a sinner as just described, let me assure you, as a dear son and humble servant of Jesus, that you can be genuinely saved today, even now, if you are ready. The nearest day tomorrow may be too late.

When on 9/10. A day before 9/11, I was on the "J" train preaching the gospel of Jesus; the last thing I said was that my listeners should make a decision that day, as they got back home before they went to bed because tomorrow might be too late. The next day would be the fateful September 11th.

After salvation, every one of us ought to begin and continue to hunger and thirst after righteousness so we may be filled. When you hunger in the physical realm, you may not be thirsty at the same time. When you thirst also, you may not be hungry at the same point. But when you both hunger and thirst, that is another story.

Regardless of how long or recently you have been saved, when you hunger and thirst after righteousness:

1. Your thirst for the pleasure of sin will be quenched by Christ's righteousness, imputed and imparted to you.
2. Your soul will pant and thirst after God as the heart pants after the brook, as in Psalm 42: 1-2.
3. You will always want more of God and will consciously seek Him more and more through His word and in prayers.
4. You will obey Him and seek to please Him, to live for Him.
5. You will not despise His teachings, His teachers. In fact, you will gravitate towards His presence.

PRACTICAL CHRISTIANITY
THE GREATEST SERMON EVER PREACHED
BLESSED ARE THE MERCIFUL… MATTHEW 5:7
By Pastor OLU FADARE

Blessed are the merciful, for they shall obtain mercy is the fifth beatitude. The book of proverb 3:3 admonishes us "Let not mercy and truth forsake you, bind them about your neck; write them on the table of your heart" Verse number 4 of the same scripture passage [proverbs 3:4] states the reward if we heed the third verse. "So shall you find favor and good understanding in the sight of God and man?" The fifth beatitude is concisely saying the same thing: "for they shall obtain mercy.

"Yes. Obtaining mercy is finding good favor. But let us consider first the subject matter: Blessed are the merciful. The merciful refers to a person or people who show mercy. Being merciful can be defined as being compassionate, pitiful, and benevolent towards others who have wronged us. Mercy is also a favorite. To be described as merciful, one has to fit into the afore - defined meaning. Let us see a practical example in the Bible. King David could have sent to have Mephibosheth, Saul's grandson, killed. Thereby eliminating any conceivable threat to his kingdom. Remember, slayed King Saul spent more than half of his reign pursuing after David's life.

Moreover, there was a long war between the house of Saul [After his death] and the house of David. Yet David was merciful to Mephibosheth by: (1) sparing his life, (2) restoring to him all the land of Saul, and (3) making him live in the palace and eat at

David's table (2 Samuel 9 1-8). In sharp contrast, being merciful or showing compassion in a wrong way or for ulterior motives is not the subject of this text. In (1 Samuel 23 19-21), the Ziphites of the wilderness of Ziph went to meet King Saul, assuring him that they would deliver David into his hands, having hidden himself in the region around Ziph. Saul blessed the Ziphites "for you have compassion on me." Again, that is not compassion but complicity. Complicity is taking part in a crime.

A few days ago, I read a news item in the New York Post of a Reverend Father who was cornered in a public hall by a prostitute, and she confessed her identity and asked for prayer. She stated bluntly that she did not ask for prayer to change her lifestyle but that she might not catch sexually transmitted diseases. According to her request, the Reverend Father was proud to say that he has been praying for her ever since (though the prostitute might be dead because the Reverend never met her again). What struck the Reverend gentleman in "compassion" was that such a woman could ever ask for prayer (regardless of the prayer point). The Reverend Father concluded that we should never look down on even the dredges of society. Readers can easily see here that the prostitute was not ignorant of the need for salvation. She just wanted easy money. That's her choice. She was not ignorant of the efficacy of prayer either. What she was ignorant of was the incongruous relationship between blessing and sin. Even if the prostitute's ignorance is permissible, what about the gross ignorance of the Reverend Father? He should be praying for her salvation (if at all he himself has salvation experience) and the mercy of God for her protection. But be not surprised that the more she's protected, the more she would like to continue in her filthy trade. The Reverend's encounter with the prostitute is reminiscent of my friend's encounter with a man in his church who pleaded for prayer from my friend, so he could be protected from law enforcement officers as he literally carried out his trade from one country to this country.

That was some eleven years ago. I was stunned at my friend's response when I reprimanded him for even seeking my advice on that. He had said, "But that's his own business, and he wants prayer on it. "It should be noted that my friend was an elder in his church. Well, it is hard to grow above your church. That man's business was drug trafficking. If my blood brother, friend, or anyone is engaging in an illegal business and wants prayer on it, God forbids that I use the right thing(prayer) in a wrong way. First, God will not answer me. Secondly, I will be a partaker of his sin. So, while I will not give him over to authorities, I will pray and agonize for his salvation. That is being merciful. Blessed are the merciful, for they shall obtain mercy. Being merciful the right way made David obtain mercy like no other person in the Bible.

UNDERSTANDING GOD

The title of this message is tricky somehow. Let me state from the onset that this title does not portend contradiction of Isaiah 40:8 that says as a conclusion that "there is no searching of His understanding". The statement in quote means no one can fathom God. But we can understand Him just as we should know Him. When adversity presses, many believers blame God for it, forgetting or doubting that God has a long hand to deliver from all woes and an outstretched hand to deliver good things to them that are in want. Are you one of those who are ready to" indict "God, so to speak, upon any slightest misfortune? I hope not. Their attitude is to blaspheme God at worst and blame Him at best. With shameless effrontery, they question: Why did God do this and that to me? Why didn't God stop this from happening? Why did God fail to answer my prayer when His word says He does answer prayers. And on and on from the ridiculous to downright silly questions. This kind of disposition should be expunged and totally removed from our mindset, for it shows clearly a lack of understanding of God and who God is. The right kind of understanding God is intrinsically comprehensive knowledge of the nature of God, His personality, and His ways. It knows that whatever happens or does not happen, He is still God and still good, independent, boundless, supreme, sovereign altogether. He can kill and make alive (1 Samuel 2:6) though He does not go around killing people. He does not disappoint His obedient children. So, it is not near apprehensive knowledge of God.

On the contrary, He protects, preserves, and provides. He is full of compassion and loving-kindness. And you know what?

He is always right. The book of Job chronicles the saga of a man under spiritual attack. The Hebrew book of Iyyob, titled as JOB in the Septuagint (a Greek language version of the Old Testament), wrestles with why bad things sometimes happen to good people. Good enough, the book of JOB also answers why. That is the reason why good people suffer afflictions. Psalm 34:19 states the obvious and the inherent hope, "Many are the afflictions of the righteous but the Lord delivers him from them all." It is actually in the book of JOB that you can have a clear comprehension that a person may be a good, God-fearing, born-again believer and still suffer like David, who not only was innocent before King Saul and entire Israel but was a National superhero and a Military General. JOB, the book makes us understand that the saga of Job was not retribution or natural consequence of sin (in fact, he was deemed perfect by God), but a direct evil machinations of Satan. Job had tasted opulence, but like a mirage, all his wealth and children were wiped out in a matter of hours. Job's three visiting friends all condemn him.

Mourners they were indeed, for they wept loudly with torn garments and dust-sprinkled heads. But comforters, they were not. It is not unheard of for Christians to pass through trials and tribulations. Our responses should not be unbridled issuance of queries to God. I would like to say that Job's words of complaints were what I call typical mourners syndrome. His mistake is of the head and not of the heart. He thought God caused all his calamity. Even then, he did not curse God and die against the erroneous counsel of his wife. His reaction should not be taken wholesale as a model for our response if affliction strikes. We should, however, be able to say like Job, "The Lord giveth and the Lord taketh away. Blessed be the name of the Lord." Do you know and have an understanding of God's personality and ways enough to avoid sinning willfully? Or do you only chorus like many do that God is a merciful God, a good God, a Holy God, a loving God without actually believing that He is exactly so? If you acknowledge the aforementioned attributes of God, then we should stand on it without wavering. Whatever happens, we should know, believe and trust that God loves us, that He is good, merciful and faithful. If you live in a state of sin without repenting and forsaking them, He is sure angry with you as the Bible says, but He loves. He loves so much that He will forgive and save you if you have not heard a personal relationship with Him. The long and short of it is that God is not wicked as Satan, as even man. That is why Paul exhorts to give thanks in everything because it is the right thing to do.

(1 Thessalonians 5:18)

HOLINESS! JUST WHAT DOES IT MEAN?

Dr. Olu Fadare

In one article, we discussed the essentiality of holiness in deliverance. To put it succinctly, to be delivered and stay delivered, free of any bondage, you must embrace holiness and walk holily. Holiness is not only a requirement for permanent deliverance but for all believers in Jesus. But the subject of holiness, just as the doctrine, is not popular. Talking from the standpoint of a Theologian, I strongly believe without fear of contradiction that the most "dreaded" single word in Christendom after hell is not even SIN. Ironically, it is HOLINESS. Very few teachers, preachers or speakers talk about sin but considerably fewer preach holiness. If you are skeptical about this claim, just undertake a simple research and practical observation by going to local churches, especially large and mega Churches, and watching National and International Christian messages on the TV, Radio, and social media for 6 months or thereabout. The result will stun you. Sure, you will hear the word sin mentioned but will hardly hear sin reproved. You will hear all the rhetoric about sin - how Jesus took our sin and nailed it on the cross, how these (I call them sneaky preachers) call themselves sinners saved by grace, how we have unmerited favor called grace in place of condemnation and judgment. There is nothing wrong with all of the above-mentioned doctrines. What is wrong and sneaky is avoiding the whole truth. They deliberately avoid scriptures like in James 1:14-15

"But every man is tempted when he is drawn away from his own lust and enticed.

Then when lust hath conceived, it bringeth forth sin, and sin when it is finished bringeth forth death."

Let's see Romans 6:1

"What shall we say then, shall we continue in sin that grace may abound? God forbid. How shall we that are dead to sin live any longer therein?" Granted, they do not teach, preach about or reprove sin. Granted, sin is too negative for them. What about holiness? The sneaky preacher will probably quote Hebrews 12:14 - FOLLOW PEACE WITH ALL MEN AND HOLINESS WITHOUT WHICH NO ONE SHALL SEE THE LORD.

They will emphasize peace and avoid explaining holiness as a non-negotiable condition of seeing the Lord. In case anyone also dreads the word holiness, I will endeavor to expatiate on it. Holiness is simply holy living or Christlike living. It is not what should be seen as unattainable. Those who do not preach it probably have no clue what it is, or they avoid it because it can make their congregation uncomfortable or scared, or it may be they know what holiness is, but they are too enmeshed in carnality to live a holy life.

Let it be known that holy living is a must for all of us from the pulpit to the pew, from preachers to the prophets, from the priest to the layman. All we have got to do is to be genuinely saved and continue in total obedience to the word of God.

HOLY LIVING AND DELIVERANCE

Dr. Olu Fadare

May I first acknowledge my readers who have displayed erudition, not only by reading this column but also by making comments, commentaries, and even asking questions? These are the people I call scholarly, well- informed, learned, intellectual. I love engaging myself in such activities as well, either writing to a Christian magazine editor or writing a comment on NY Daily News columnist article. The first person who responded to my first article on Christianity is a Nigerian economist residing in New Jersey but working in Queens New York. He asked a relevant question on which he wanted to know my stand. He is a Muslim who converted to Christianity 27 years or so ago. Since his contact, I have heard from others. In Queens, NY a woman of God who said she was much blessed. She wrote her comments on WhatsApp last May. She wrote: "I love this write up. I'm excited reading this. These are words of a regenerated BELIEVER, a disciple and an Apostle of JESUS Christ, written in truth and with boldness and clarity. God bless you sir." Another Christian woman, a Ghanaian American, called for deliverance and counseling. The purpose of this column is to bring more awareness to the importance of deliverance and encourage people to seek it. One of the people who called was amazed that the problem of oppression and spirit possession I wrote about perfectly described her problem. According to her, she believed that God would use the LIVING GOD MIRACLE MINISTRY to deliver her totally. I assured her that by the power of The Living God, she will be free and that our healing and deliverance Ministry is and will always remain free of charge. Thank God for people who had come from across New York City, Long Island, New Jersey, and as far as the state of Vermont for either healing or deliverance. Amazing things God is doing.

This brings me to a pertinent question: Why is it that many endlessly go through deliverance back to back and are never totally free? The reason is no brainer at all. First, some Ministries or Churches out there claim to be deliverance ministries but actually do not minister deliverance either in mass or one on one. They do not even know how to cast out a single spirit, let alone multitudes of them. It might be they have no clue what deliverance is. Secondly, some use diabolic means and employ unbiblical rituals in the process. What we see is a travesty of core doctrine resulting in more bondage for the oppressed. Thirdly, it may be a case of physician healing thyself. The person ministering deliverance might need deliverance himself. Fourthly, the deliverance minister might be living in sin, or the oppressed person might be living in unrepented sin, immorality, uncontrolled anger, unforgiveness, pride, covetousness, and so on. These works of the flesh defy a man. For deliverance to be effective and permanent, both the minister and the one receiving deliverance must embrace holy living. (Hebrew 12:14-15)

A Christian woman who prayed and endured for years for her husband to be saved finally had her prayers answered. But she, on her part, struggled with deliverance on and off. One day, she told me, "Brother, now I know that a person cannot be totally free without holiness." I was shocked that she knew this truth - because many do not know it. Without holy living after deliverance, there is that propensity for the stronger return of spirits. (Matthew 12:43).

Dr. Olusola Fadare is the senior pastor of LIVING GOD MIRACLE MINISTRY,172-02 Jamaica Ave. Jamaica, NY (917)535-5462

MORE ON HOLINESS

In the last issue titled, Holiness! JUST WHAT DOES IT MEAN?" I dwelt on this subject as a core biblical and Christian doctrine, endeavoring to make it simple without trivializing or extenuating its essentiality. Yes, it is simple, but not simplistic. It is not an idea, an opinion, or a hypothesis which are subject to arguments and debates. Holiness is a doctrine, and it is required and commanded by God. And it has a universal application as far as Christianity and Christians are concerned. In other words, it is non- denominational.

Not only is it for all denominational and non- denominational churches, but it is also required of all Christians. If a church is not Bible preaching (the whole Bible), gospel-preaching, and Christ-believing church, then holiness is not expected of them, and it is not required. Why not? The answer is because such one is not a church. Yes, it can have a nice, good, and fanciful name, but it is not part of the body of Christ. In the same vein, anyone who has not been born again (saved) is not mandated to embrace holiness or be holy. No, he or she must first be born again. In other words, all are called to be born again, not to be holy. But all born-again Christians are called to be holy.

It is a clarion call for all people of God, for individuals, and for Nations. The Lord God Almighty first called 'Abram' out in Genesis chapter 12. He was called out from his family and father's house to a life of separation, knowledge, and obedience to God. It was not until chapter 17 that God called him to be perfect (holy, complete). He had been what you could now call a child of God, a believer for fifteen years from age 75 to 90. But when he was 90, fifteen years after the first call, God was like saying, "You know, you have known me. I know you obey me; I know you have separated yourself from idolatry and traditions of men. But I want you to walk with me far and to be complete. For that, you will need to walk perfectly (holily). With the new spiritual experience, you will be a totally different person from when a decade or so ago you asked Sarah, your wife, to say she was your sister if the Egyptians asked who she was." I am not saying God told him all these things, but that could have been their dialogue or the motive behind God's appearance to Abram, introducing Himself as the Almighty God and that Abram should walk before Him and be perfect (Genesis 17:1).

Speaking to a whole Nation of Israel, God said, "And you shall be holy men unto me," as in the first part of Exodus 22:31. Also, in Leviticus, the Lord commanded the Israelites to be holy because he is a Holy God (Leviticus 11:44-45). In 1 Peter 1:15-17, Peter in the New Testament wrote to all the body of Christ that were then scattered all over the land of Palestine and beyond; the same call, the same message: Be holy. Backing up to verse 14, he addressed them as obedient children. But in verses 15 to 17, he spelled out the end of it: Be holy. Our salvation aims to walk with God here on earth and continue the relationship in heaven. So salvation is not the end; It is the means to an end. May I emphasize now, as I pointed out in the last message, that holiness should not be a dreadful word or some unattainable goal as some see it? It is simply holy living or Christlike living. This holy living is rooted in the love of God and love for all people, more especially for the brethren in the faith. When you are genuinely saved, you will separate yourself from sinful and vain lifestyles and people or things that embody sin and worldliness. This is physical sanctification. Then you need to be spiritually sanctified as well, meaning you get rid of things that defy the body, mind, and spirit - fornication, adultery, idolatry, sensual things (pornography in magazines or moving pictures), filthy habits, lies, profane expressions, uncontrolled anger, unforgiveness, hatred, greed and so on.

As you then ask Jesus to cleanse you in the inner man, you will be deemed sanctified and holy. The life you will then live without these works of the flesh will be clean, holy life.

As a result, you would have experienced what a well-informed teacher and Christian leader called spirit born, spirit formed, and spirit-led.

CONSECRATION OR COMPROMISE?

Our Lord Jesus Christ saw the prevalence of evil when he walked the streets of the regions of Galilee, Judea, and beyond, two thousand plus years ago. As He preached and taught, he called a spade a spade, so to speak. He saw a generation that was negatively distinct from previous generations of God-loving, God-fearing people. In Mark 8:38, Jesus called them adulterous generation. In Luke 3:7, they were referred to as a generation of vipers by John the Baptist. In Luke 11:29, Jesus called them an evil generation, and in Matthew 17:17, he also used strong language, calling them faithless and perverse generations.

Imagine what Jesus would call this generation. What would you call a generation of people that kills upon the slightest provocation, that lives by the gun and dies by the gun, that sadistically kills, steals, maim and destroy without a minuscule of remorse? A generation of people that hate others with irrevocable, absolute, and perfect hatred that their only recourse is to kill even if they will have to kill themselves after. This is a generation that calls evil good and good evil that euphemistically call abomination lifestyle and assign any other nomenclature to sin because the word "sin" to them is dead. That is the bane of the post-modern world we are living in.

Years ago, I gave a speech in which I said prophetically that though we are in the age of information, as they say, you are all welcome to the age of terrorism. Active shooting incidents come under the umbrella of terrorism. Whether it is homegrown or not, complicity involves two or more attackers or a lone wolf. It does not also matter if such acts of terrorism have no political or religious cloak. So long as it targets the public, a section of the public, or a representation of the same, and so long as it is unleashed to terrorize.

So what is the panacea for the ills of society? - the individual hatred, acts of violence, acts of terror, gross ungodliness, utter moral collapse, perpetrated and being perpetuated by this generation, which the Lord Jesus would have called "Satanic or anti- Christ." JESUS is the answer. There is a grave need for society to look for the answer in Christ Jesus. He self-declared that He is the way, the truth, and the life (John 14:6), and nobody comes to the father (that is, God) but only through Him (Jesus). People of different religions have had spiritual encounters with Jesus through dreams, visions, and even physical appearances. Their lives will never be the same. They now know Jesus is real, that He is the son of the Living God, who we can call like father, like son, chip of the old block, the true express image of God as the Bible puts it. Let true stories of encounters/appearances by Jesus be spread, let Christians challenge unbelieving others to call upon Jesus. He will show Himself to them. The encounters with Jesus are getting more widespread because Jesus' glorious return is imminent. This is the end of the end, not the beginning of the end. This is the last page of the Book of the world. Soon we will get to the last paragraph and then the last sentence before the last period stops everything and the book is closed.

As for us, the followers of Christ, who have known the truth, there are two things to do: (1) Put your house in order and (2) preach Christ and not just prosperity. Specializing and concentrating on prosperity is an eternal diversion from the truth and person of Jesus and His gospel. The aim of such exercises is to raise, and amass money and wealth for the preachers. Do not be deceived; there is nothing like the prosperity gospel because it is not a gospel.

How do we put our house in order? It starts with examining your own salvation, making sure you are solidly in Christ Jesus (2 Corinthians 5:17). "If anyone is in Christ Jesus, he is a new creature, old things are passed away, behold all things have become new." If almost all things have become new in you, you still have some repentance or surrender to do.

All things must become new. If people around you and the beings in the spirit realms, satan and his cohorts the demons, and God and His Angels don't see you as a genuine Christian, you are not. Perhaps you have slacked up. The heavens and even the demons testified of Jesus, and Peter and Paul in the Bible (Acts 19 vs. 11-18).

If you are sure you are still much in the faith, then be careful of compromise. Avoid compromising the core of your Christian doctrine, which is in TRUTH. A churchgoer who is still all over the place going from one woman to another or man to another man (if she is a woman) is in the same group as a born-again believer who is preying on just one innocent lady. By all means, don't see anything as too little or insignificant. No little lie, no little sin, no once in a while sinning. The sure way is not to compromise but to consecrate. Consecration includes giving yourself to prayers and reading of the word. Fasting on a regular basis, and of course consecrating some days or an entire weekend to be in the presence of God. Doing this shows hunger for and love of God in you.

Dr. Olu Fadare is a teacher, preacher, theologian, and senior pastor of Living God Miracle Ministry, a healing/ deliverance church. Located at 172-02 Jamaica Ave, Queens, NY. He can be reached at (917) 535-5462 for prayer, counseling, and deliverance.

RESURRECTION POWER IS IN THE AIR
PASTOR FADARE

The news should send shock waves across the entire spectrum of society. At least the entirety of the body of Christ called the church. It is not fake news. It is real - the news that Brooklyn D.A (District Attorney), an influential man with a powerful office, will support decriminalization of prostitution. He publicly said it. His statement simply translates to promoting decriminalization of the so-called oldest profession in the world. Stated more simply, he is promoting the legalization of open prostitution just like the current legalization of recreational marijuana. Alarming! Terrifying! Are not strong enough to express the shock. If legalized (and anything goes in our society now), a fatal blow would have been dealt the already moral free fall we are now witnessing. The repercussion would then be a total, absolute - irrevocable demise of the crumbling moral values of the society. The aura of darkness will usher in an era of perpetual darkness that will so morbidly permeate the society that good would be perceived as evil, righteousness as sin, and truth as profanity. In the blackness of the darkness that would alter the sensibilities of men, advocates would rise and champion evil courses.

What about banning marriages because there is unprecedented high rate of divorce, and technically it costs the government millions of dollars annually? What about people who are into bestiality advocating secret but legal marriage with their lover animals? What about legalizing polygamy so long as there are no more than three wives to a man, so no woman would be spouseless. Then some women's equal rights advocates would voice for women's right to marry two or three husbands.

The scenarios described above are far-fetched, but with the socio-political landscape, as it is, they could happen. We are this close to total moral collapse. Morbid conscience begets moral collapse. Christian and Religious people everywhere wake up, articulate, and fight a good fight for your posterity and your faith.

Talking about faith, the commemoration of the resurrection of our Lord Jesus Christ, commonly called Easter Sunday, is April 21st this year of our Lord 2019. Forget about the controversial story of the origin of Easter. It is the devil's tactic of polarizing the church. Let us keep on celebrating the resurrection of our Lord Jesus. Some of the justification for the celebration of the resurrection is: Without the resurrection of Jesus, the crucifixion would be absolutely meaningless. If Jesus did not rise, there is also no hope for us as men, and as Christians. 1 Corinthians 15:19 says, if in this life only we have hope in Christ, we are of all men most miserable. If Christ has not risen, then the preaching of the cross of Christ is vain, and our Christian faith is vain (1 Corinthians 15:14).

If Christ has not risen, we will still be in our sins, and those that died in Christ will have perished. Not only did Christ rise from the dead, but there will also be a resurrection of the dead - all people that have died from Adam, the first man to the last man that will die. Some will go to everlasting life, while some will go to everlasting shame. (Daniel 12:2).

Two great scriptures put a stamp of finality to second- guessing of the doctrine of resurrection: 1 Corinthians 15:3-8 and 1 John 5:13. The latter also assures believers that eternal life is theirs. If you are not a born again Christian, the latter scripture is your promise too if you can acknowledge now that you have sinned in your life, that you are a sinner who sins and that you believe Jesus Christ is the son of the living God who came to the world to save sinners like you. Ask for forgiveness of your sins, be sorry for them. Think of what the Bible says of the penalty (or pay) for sins: death. This is eternal separation from God and heaven forever and ever, and the immediate sentence to hell fire after death. After repenting and determining to turn away from life of sin and godlessness, then invite Jesus to your life to be your savior and Lord whose word (Bible) you will obey. Invite His spirit to be in you so you can be transformed spiritually. Once you have done this, you will be regarded as saved or born again right away. Then the promise in First John chapter 5 verse 13 is yours. All you need do going forward is to study the Bible like LIFE APPLICATION BIBLE and find a Bible preaching, strong prayerful church to attend regularly. Dare not skip church to go and make extra money. That day of worship is the Lord's. My last justification for the celebration of Jesus' resurrection is that it is the greatest event of all time. Nothing that ever happened since the world began is greater. Nothing

Another great, momentous event that parallels that will soon happen. DO NOT MISS IT. It is what the Bible describes as the glorious appearance of the great God and our savior Jesus Christ. It is called "The Rapture" by Christians. In one of my article, I promised I would share my second regret as a young Christian decades ago. And that is the fact that I was not John the Baptist who was the forerunner of Christ. Honestly, I wished I was John, the only person in this world ever to be the forerunner of Christ. He was described by Jesus as the greatest man ever born. Why? Because he was the only forerunner, who heralded the 1st coming of Jesus. He introduced Jesus to the world. Oh, I missed being John. Did you ever share my regret? Mind you, I was a naive, young Christian. But then Jesus not only said that the least in the kingdom of God is greater than John (when he was on earth). I was only partially pleased with that assurance until the spirit of God spoke to my heart, "One person heralded the first coming, many, including you, can herald the second coming." Amen! That means you and I have the same privilege John had, the same task. He was the forerunner of the 1st coming. You and I are the forerunners of the 2nd coming. Yes, you can be if you can witness Christ leading people to salvation by the grace of Jesus. Are you excited about being a forerunner? You better be. May the power of resurrection quicken every dead thing in your life. Amen.

BLESSED
PASTOR FADARE

We all used the word "Bless" extravagantly. We are in a culture and generation that uses words, words, and words. Coupled with that is the information age that we are in. Inherent in the words that people speak are curses and profanities. In fact, people use them with impunity. You hear handsome men, pretty women, educated and apparently decent folks use curses, and profane words for such have become part of their daily vocabulary. I will not spare even "Christians," who I will euphemistically call church people. Oh, many of us use curse words with reckless abandon. Have you noticed people saying, "excuse me" or "excuse my language," after such indecent effusion?

Handsomeness and prettiness are incongruous with dirty verbal profane-ness; talk less of such profanities oozing from a supposedly clean, holy vessel. Unfortunately, many Christians, including titled ministers, do not understand or are careless or are uncommitted to holy living. Do we read in vain the scriptures that say: "The wicked is snared by transgression of his lips: but the just shall come out of trouble."? (Proverbs 12:13) KJV "A man shall be satisfied with good by the fruit of his mouth; and the recompense of a man's hands shall be rendered unto him." (Proverbs 12:14) KJV

Did not our Lord Jesus warn that every idle word spoken by a man, he shall give an account of it on the day of judgment?

"For by thy words thou (you) shall be justified, and by thy words thou shall be condemned." (Matthew 12:37)

In contrast, people use the word "bless" also profusely, and so rampantly that it has become casual and commonplace. The word does not even convey what it means any longer. For instance, "God bless you" is not a prayer. It does not mean the person spoken to is blessed or will be blessed. We now have an endless deluge of blessings and "prayers" daily flooding social media. Jesus has not called us or mandated us primarily to be 'blessers'. He mandated us to be witnesses and ambassadors of Him. The current prevalence of prayers deluge all over social media is an indication of misplaced priority. It has no parallel in the Bible or in the history of the church. The epistles - Pauline, pastoral, and all the apostolic epistles usually start with general greetings or a line of a prayer. Then it goes into the substance - the rationales for writing. It may be exhortations, core doctrines, reproof, admonition, or a clarion call for repentance. The contents of these writings have been transforming lives since their canonical inception.

Even in the Pentateuch's Deuteronomy 28th and Leviticus 26th, where blessings were profusely pronounced on the Israelites, the blessings were conditional. This writer is not saying that prayers directed to people on social media are anathema to me, but you know fully well if you possess some spiritual knowledge that it does not work that way. All biblical blessings are conditional - on obedience to God's words and godly living. I say again, as I have written before on this column, those originators of these spurious prayers and pseudo-blessings should exhort their contacts and others to love God, their neighbors, and especially fellow believers. They should remind them of the saving grace of Jesus for salvation and the mandated task of spreading the gospel through all avenues and by all means necessary. That is the right way to bless people. That is the enduring blessing of the soul. When the soul prospers, other things will follow.

There are good, knowledgeable Christians out there who get it right. I got this clip on "WhatsApp" forwarded to a brother in the church who forwarded it to me: "Father you sent your son into this world not to condemn it but to save it. Teach me today O God how to be in this world, how to live in community and yet avoid the contamination of selfishness and greed, and the poison of pride and resentment. Open my eyes that I may see others with Your eyes and mold my heart that it may always be receptive to Your word. Father I would be the first to admit that taking up this cross daily is not easy, so strengthen me where I am weak, replace my fear with faith and in all things, help me to remember that love will conquer all." Another one, just yesterday. "Papa God, You said I should not let my heart be troubled and that I should put my faith in You. Thanks for that assurance today, thanks for that faithfulness to me, Your providence, Your generosity, Your protection and guidance. How can I ever repay You O God? If I had ten thousand tongues it still would not be enough to sing Your praises. Today O God, all I can offer is my broken sinful self, a heart that believes in tomorrow. May my life be a living sacrifice to You today, and every day of my life."

If you are filled with the spirit of God, in fact, if you have the spirit of God, to say the least, you will agree with me that these two write-ups are perfect examples of how we, ministers and believers can touch lives proactively and positively while we, with our prayers back it up to transform lives. The two writers quoted have just done how social media should be used by believers to impact lives for Jesus. It's like modern psalmists writing down their thoughts and inspirations. That is the blessing.

Talking about true blessings, I have been reminded of the beatitudes of the sermon on the mount preached by the Lord Jesus Christ as documented in the book of Matthew Chapter 5. The word blessed keep showing up nine times, from Verses 3- 11. Every new sentence is a doctrine and every doctrines comes with the unique word, called blessed.

The true blessing is not when you say 'bless you' to a person or a person says it to you. As a matter of fact, a task become a formal greeting as common place as the word, "thank you." We say, thank you when an obligation is perform or a request is granted and even before the action is perform. When we express gratitude, with thanks the receiver of thanks in return says thank you back often times instead of the traditional "you're welcome." Bless you if likewise expression that has, like thank you lost its meaning. Even when people prefix it with God bless you it's just an expression of politeness. "Thank you for returning my call, God bless you, for instance, just not translate to the person wished them bless or with be. True blessing, which means, favor, is actually tied to obedience and performance of spiritual exercise or action that portends.

AMERICA! CHURCH OR CONVENIENCE?

DR. OLU FADARE

By the grace of God, this column is back after a few weeks of vacation in Nigeria. Did I say vacation? It was not a vacation per se, but my annual trip for ministerial help and to oversee an arm of our church, The Living God Miracle Ministry at Ibadan, Nigeria. I thank God for His work at our branch in Nigeria. While I had ample time preaching, teaching, ministering deliverance, and healing with questions and answer sessions, I also had the privilege to participate in evangelistic outreach.

Yes, it is a privilege to witness Christ. We are not doing Christ a favor by doing so. Though we are commanded to witness Christ, it is still a privilege in the sense that the person, that is, the believer witnessing Christ, must have himself or herself been translated from darkness into the marvelous light of Christ (Colossians 1:13).

His obedience to the great commission (Mark 16:15-16) is predicated on his own regeneration, and it parallels Christ's ministering effort to rescue the perishing from HELL. In other words, it is the continuation of Jesus' teachings and cries for the salvation of souls. The believer who witnesses is occupying until Jesus returns.

He is an ambassador of Jesus. The actual salvation of souls and the ultimate sacrifice on the cross has no parallel. This cannot be repeated, duplicated, or replicated by anyone's efforts. It is solely Christ's.

For over ten years of my ministering in Nigeria - tent revivals, church revivals/ministration, and street evangelism, I have seen healing miracles, deliverance miracles, and salvation of souls, including the conversion from other religions to the Christian faith. Amazing! To God be the glory, great things He has done. Though I have seen these things and had rejoiced with the beneficiaries of His miracles, yet never had I been so thrilled seeing the matchless zeal of brethren in Nigeria in terms of corporate fasting, church attendance, including weekday services, generous giving, exuberant, spirited praise and worship, vibrant warfare prayers and focused undistracted attention.

These ideals and disciplined practices are universally visibly missing in American churches. I equate the American church with what has become a cultural paradigm in the fabric of the American economy: The Convenience Store. It has essentially become the quintessential model of the American church. The convenience store is close to your home and has easy access in and out. The convenience store stocks your needs from a cold bottle of juice to a piece of banana. The convenience store has your budget in mind.

You can do all of your shopping in a convenience store and be out in 10 minutes, whereas in a supermarket, you are stuck in one aisle straining your neck looking for items. Can you not find your item in a convenience store? Be rest assured someone will lead you to it or pick it up for you, all for your convenience.

This is the description of the typical American Church. Everything has been designed and put in place for your convenience. Air conditioning has replaced fans even when it is not all that warm; otherwise, congregants would walk out. The sermon should not be longer than 30 minutes; otherwise, half the Church would be napping in their seats while the other half would be trafficking back and forth to the bathrooms. If the parking lot is full, and the attendant/usher happens to motion with a wave that the parking lot is full or he places a sign up stating so, some would back up in in a fury and head straight back home in self-deluded retaliation. If some congregants get to Church in the morning and are always late, and it happens that their favorite seats are taken, they become visibly upset with both the usher and the usurper of their seats, perhaps expressing their indignation verbally, thereby distracting members. The on-looking pastor or elder must not say a word, or else the "offended" member would find a more convenient church and take with him or her all the members she had invited since he or she had joined the Church.

Finally, if the pastor called for a corporate fast, he would have to fast first for three days or so, against the probability of any member who could be tempted to sue the Church for malnutrition, ulcer, stomach ache, or any related ailment incidental to skipping meals. So the pastor, in all wisdom, would declare a corporate fast or partial corporate fast such as skipping just lunch, eating only soft or liquid foods during the day, eating everything but avoiding cakes and ice cream only. Yet, many will still not participate because they have not disciplined their flesh against their cravings and indulgences for over a decade of their Christian experience. That, again, is the picture of the American Church.

In all honesty, the Church in Nigeria is far from being a convenience church. Hundreds of preachers in America and elsewhere can attest to this fact. I have read their correspondence, attended their Ministry conventions and International conventions going back two decades, and still attending. I have had how these pastors, bishops, and evangelists talk about the African Church generally and the Nigerian Church in particular, about the brethren, about their incomparable fiery prayers, their tenacity, sheer ruggedness, fixation with mountain trips prayers, their prodigiously generous praise-worship sessions expressed in peculiar dance moves and clappings for the Almighty and of course the nomenclature of the Christian identity of their posterity. Names like PECULIAR FAITH, ANOINTING, ZION, PROMISE, OBEDIENCE, FAVOR, KING DAVID and so on. At his church conference, one American pastor based in Baton Rouge told us in Pelham, Westchester County, NY, about how the brethren in Nigeria would be praying, calling FIRE! FIRE! Another big pastor spoke somewhere else of how he went to Nigeria, and how he felt like he just started learning Ministry stuff among giants of faith.

All these are a testimony of the level of zeal for and love of God in the Nigeria Church. It is far from being a community of faith whose Church had been designed for their convenience. Living far away or nearby, poor or broke, brethren will find their way to Church. Perhaps that is why the Nigerian Church is at the forefront of global Christian exploits and leadership. Look at phenomenal auditoriums, million souls' convention gatherings, multi-acres of ministry campgrounds that have become towns and cities on their own, and thousands of healings and deliverance miracles happening from time to time. No wonder Nigeria is fast becoming the Mecca of the global Christian faith. We Ministers of the gospel in America (of African descent) must be dedicated, committed to faithfully keep the torch burning. Let us not compromise or succumb to the characteristics of convenience. We must be focused, full gospel preaching, humble and heavenly-minded, and serve with these Christian virtues and ideals.

Olu Fadare is a writer, theologian, and senior pastor of the Living God ministries. He ministers healings and deliverance and can be reached at 9175355462 or at Olusolafad@aol.com.

OF LIGHT WEIGHTS AND THE SKILLFUL

The "ides" of March have come," Caesar said mockingly to the soothsayer in Shakespeare's classic play "Julius CAESAR," dismissing the warnings of certain death on the 15th of March called the "ides of March."

"But not gone, Caesar," the soothsayer countered. He had earlier warned Caesar long before the ides of March. Relax, this is not March. Neither is it December; This is January 2019. 2018 is gone, forever. Glory to God! for another year. Great things He has done for us all. Even an ingrate will always see what God has done for him or her. To be thankful to God? To an ingrate, that is another thing entirely. While countless born-again Christians and nominal Christians across the entire spectrum of the Christian community thanked God for everything, from protection and preservation, to blessings and breakthroughs, countless others (mostly non-Christians) are just thankful. Such thankfulness is not predicated by the word "God," as in "we are thankful" instead of we are thankful to God. Similar things like, "we are grateful to see another year." Grateful to who? You might ask. Apostle Paul in 1 Corinthians 15:57 wrote, "But thanks be to God, who gives us the victory through our Lord Jesus Christ." To be candid, most Muslims even attribute their gratitude to their "ALLAH." But outside of these two groups are the adherents of the Jewish faith. They consciously acknowledge the God of Abraham, Isaac, and Jacob in verbalizing their gratitude. Outside of these three religious groups are countless others who are never thankful or are thankful to no one, man, or deity. These are whatever name or description you give to them - freewill thinkers, proud persons, pagans, atheists. They may be thankful for anything in life, health, family. Yes, thankful "for" but not "to". That is the crux of the matter.

And talking of atheists, when they say they do not believe in God, they are really saying that they do not want God in their lives. A common-sense definition of an atheist is not one who does not believe in God but one who does not want God in his life. Let us be realistic. Even the fool in Psalm 14-1 Knows there is God in his mind

NEO-CHRISTIAN TREND

I see a new trend among Christians. It started from the pulpit and has pervaded the body of Christ to a large extent. This season is particularly ripe for it. They inundate their WhatsApp and Facebook friends and followers with a plethora of prayer wishes, profusely quoting from the scripture. They may even indirectly curse or threaten anyone who fails to share their sentiments with other social media audiences. Throughout the year, you will continue to be deluged with scores of vague prayers written and spoken by so-called prophets, pastors, Evangelists, laymen, and nominal Christians across all the denominations. These I call spiritual lightweights. Folks, there is something spiritually wrong with the person who posts prayers on social media consistently without ever telling their followers, viewers, or readers about salvation, the efficacy of the cross of Christ, the need to be sanctified and committed to holy living, personal prayer life and fasting, the need to not only read, study and meditate on the word of God, the Bible. But to live by it as we live by food daily (Luke 4:4). They never encourage or pray for their audience to flee all manners of sin or warn about worldliness that has so much infiltrated the Church, making the Church so worldly. They never talk about challenging or encouraging their audience to strive to witness and lead unbelievers to the cross. What about being heaven-minded or the blessed hope of the imminent return of Christ. The spiritual landscape now is that the Church is so worldly and the world is so Churchy that it will take you a discerning spirit to know who belongs to which Real Christians have become endangered species, so to speak. If Christians, including ministers of the gospel, must post prayers on social media, why not pray on the aforementioned old-time Religion culture. A typical one could be: This new year and all of 2019, with the help of the Holy Spirit, you will not only worship the Lord God in truth and in spirit but seek him more for a more intimate way by spending quality time in prayer and in the word. May you set your affection and priority pursuit on the things above (heavenly) more than the things beneath (earthly).

Another could be: Let your faith be strong and stronger from this year going forward, so much that you will believe God for answered prayers. If you pray in faith and according to His will, He will surely answer your prayers. Do not cease trusting Him because He is a good God who wants good, beneficial things for you. It may be a little delayed, but he will not deny you. Your expectations shall not be cut off. If all you post is about the death of your enemies and all the goodies possession and similar things, the devil is already diverting you with his diversionary tactics. You will share that kind of prayer to scores of others, and the end result is that we in the Christian circle have become a bunch of enemy-fearing, worldliness-loving, vanity-pursuing carnal people. Do not be a lightweight like them. There are many, many that the Lord has not called but have "called" themselves as Reverends, Pastors, Prophets, and Prophetesses. Many others have been truly called to ministry within the five-fold ministry.

Many in this group of the Lord told me while away in Santa Rosa, Florida, about six years ago, that he has called them, but many of them had gone after their own way to make themselves famous and chase after their own gains. In other words, they had made themselves the center of attention and attraction, cultivating a personality cult for themselves and commercializing the gospel. These "servants" of God might be celebrities, little-known folks, or just start-ups. These are the ones you see or read on the T.V and on social media serving their own agenda. They dish out bogus prayers and prophecies. They are all over the place. Even if their prophecies are true and their prayers biblical, the question remains: What is their motive? Do they expect consultation so they can charge money for their "services," or just a way of manipulation? The Lord said, "You have received freely, give freely." What the Lord has sent us to do is to preach the gospel. You may be a prophet or a singer/worshipper. Your calling should revolve around the gospel of salvation. Period.

About 4 years ago. During our Church's 7 day fasting/praying period, our Lord Jesus appeared to a sister, telling her similar things about his servants who think they are serving God but have gone their own way of fame-seeking and greed. "Would you like to know about your own pastor?" The Lord asked. She was glad to know that her pastor, my humble self is not like that. Many servants of God have not deviated from the gospel committed to us by Jesus Christ. Our job is to project Jesus and hide behind Him, to proclaim the good news and invite people to accept Jesus by repenting of their ungodly ways and live for Jesus forevermore and send out prayers to the end that they may not falter or slack back and to trust in God in the time of trial and when things seem to fall apart.

So readers, may your health, soul, and all things concerning you prosper this year going forward. May you have personal encounter after encounter with Jesus in prayers and worship, in Church and in your homes. May you be filled and live and walk in the spirit evermore. May you never be tired of seeking Jesus for more intimacy. May you have the Holy Ghost boldness to share your Christian experience with others and lead them to Christ. May you live to serve Him. Amen. If you are not sure you are born again, why won't you just find a place to kneel down or bow your head and confess your sins to Jesus, who died for us all? Invite His spirit to come to you. Accept Him as savior and Lord. If you do this heartily, you are what is called "born again."

Dr. Olu Fadare is the senior Pastor of Living God Miracle Ministry (for healing and deliverance).
Can be reached at (917) 535 5462.

RELIGION

Practical Christianity

THE GREATEST QUESTIONS EVER ASKED

An inquisitive reader will wonder what the greatest questions ever asked could be and what criteria would designate them as the greatest speaking spiritually, they are not only the greatest but the most crucial. So in this piece, I will endeavor to present with simplicity the most relevant, pertinent personal, and timeless questions in the Bible, howbeit in all of the world. I am, in effect, stating without equivocation that no one can shy away from the daunting reality of this question. Whether it is you, the reader, or your friends and loved ones, your neighbors, any groupings of people, or an unknown aggregate of people, incidentally or accidentally gathering together for an uncommon interest. Anyone anywhere on earth. The first question is asked in the book of Hebrew chapter 2 verse 3,

"How shall we escape if we neglect so great a salvation?"

Escape from what? Escape from condemnation from the guilt and deadliness of sin and from hellfire. In short, from spiritual and eternal death, the latter being eternal separation from God forever and ever. The next similar question comes from the book of Acts. 16:30, asked by the Philippian jailer from the two men of God who were under his guard in prison. Paul and Silas had spent the night singing and praising God when suddenly an earthquake rumbled through the whole building, flinging the iron prison doors open and miraculously breaking the men's bands. "Sirs, what must I do to be saved?" If you have not been saved, and living a Christlike (Christian) life, there is no more urgent, crucial question than this. All other questions of life – who should I marry, what college should I go to, what career should I choose, which house should I purchase, and so on - all these pale in comparison to: "What shall I do to be saved?." Well, the answer that came spontaneously over two thousand years ago is the same timeless answer today: Believe in the Lord Jesus, and you shall be saved and your house. I am also reiterating the same biblical truth. Believe that Jesus is the Son of God and God the Son, that He was incarnated and came to this earth to self sacrifice Himself by the shedding of His precious, efficacious blood, for without that shedding of His blood, there cannot be remission or forgiveness of sin. You must believe that the same who died was also buried and resurrected. 1 COR 15:3-4 states it in a succinct way. "For I delivered unto you first of all that which I also received." how that Christ died for our sins according to the scriptures. And that He was buried, and that He rose again the third day according to the scriptures. Our third question was asked by Pilate, who unfortunately did not wait for an answer from Jesus before he went straight up to confer and confess to the Jews that Jesus was faultless, "What is truth?"

The biblical account in - the book of John chapter 18 of the encounter between Our Lord Jesus and Pilate points out that every one that is of the truth hears Jesus' voice. Against this backdrop, Pilate's question was prompted. He probably intended a rhetorical question. But this is not. It is a fundamental one. Many good-intentioned people have believed in error. But the road to hell is paved with good intentions. Jesus is the truth. The totality of the word of God is the truth - biblical doctrines as opposed to sectarian doctrines, every revelation of God, self-declarations of Jesus, biblical historical facts, and the prophecies. The last of our great and crucial questions were also asked during an encounter with Jesus. Nicodemus in John's chapter. 3 verse 4: "How can a man be born {again} when he is old?" Nicodemus wondered if he would have to enter his mother's womb again and be born. Years ago, in 1990, I gave a coworker a ride in the car from Manhattan to Brooklyn.

It was an opportunity for me to witness Christ to him. When I mentioned the word salvation, he asked in innocent ignorance, "Is it The Salvation Army?" This is to say that countless people do not even have a clue to what is being born again. It is incumbent on us and mandatory as well that we have to propagate the gospel. How can a man be born again? According to Nicodemus, an important public figure in his days, it is a supernatural experience, as the Lord explained in the same passage of the scripture. It is not a mental accent of believing that Jesus is the son of God for the devil himself believes and even trembles, the Bible says. To be born again or be saved, you must acknowledge you are a sinner that needs help and mercy and that you cannot save yourself, no matter how nice, generous, or prayerful you may be. Then begin to verbally confess your sins, asking for forgiveness. In that state of contrition, be willing to repent, forsaking those sins and that state of sin. Believe the word of God, and that is, the Bible – that Jesus, the son of God, died for your sin, and He is resurrected in glory. Ask Jesus to come into your life and be your savior and Lord. As you do this or guide someone through this, you or that person will be called born again because you will begin to see a transformation in your life as you just got born again by faith and the grace of Jesus Christ. By doing this, you will no longer be indebted to the questions aforementioned.

Think about this, for the questions are not rhetorical questions. They have to be answered by our decision to accept Jesus as savior and Lord. It is your choice, but if you choose not to, you will face the disagreeable, unimaginable consequence of your unwise choice.

BOOK SUMMARY

This book concerns what should concern every minister of God and every true child of God. Who Jesus is and who He is not. Is the Christian faith something to be practiced with ease and convenience? Does every Christian know whether or not Christians, Muslims, Buddhists, Hinduists, etc., serve the same God? These and many other essays and sermons in this book address a variety of fundamental biblical truths. Unfortunately, some Christian believers are of the opinion that religion is personal, that God accepts everyone, and that the religion that you practice is your own way of serving God and that we should not judge. Well, they should know that speaking the truth and affirming and proclaiming the same is not passing judgment. Read each of these topical sermons and essays to broaden your knowledge and ignite your zeal.

www.ingramcontent.com/pod-product-compliance
Lightning Source LLC
LaVergne TN
LVHW021239080526
838199LV00088B/5171